One Hidden Stuff

One Hidden Stuff

BARBARA RAS

PENGUIN POETS

PENGUIN BOOKS

Published by the Penguin Group

Penguin Group (USA) Inc., 375 Hudson Street, New York, New York 10014, U.S.A.

Penguin Group (Canada), 90 Eglinton Avenue East, Suite 700, Toronto, Ontario, Canada M4P 2Y3 (a division of Pearson Penguin Canada Inc.)

Penguin Books Ltd, 80 Strand, London WC2R 0RL, England

Penguin Ireland, 25 St Stephen's Green, Dublin 2, Ireland (a division of Penguin Books Ltd)

Penguin Group (Australia), 250 Camberwell Road, Camberwell, Victoria 3124, Australia (a division of Pearson Australia Group Pty Ltd)

Penguin Books India Pvt Ltd, 11 Community Centre, Panchsheel Park, New Delhi – 110 017, India

Penguin Group (NZ), cnr Airborne and Rosedale Roads, Albany, Auckland 1310, New Zealand (a division of Pearson New Zealand Ltd)

Penguin Books (South Africa) (Pty) Ltd, 24 Sturdee Avenue, Rosebank, Johannesburg 2196, South Africa

Penguin Books Ltd, Registered Offices:
80 Strand, London WC2R 0RL, England

First published in Penguin Books 2006

10 9 8 7 6 5 4 3 2 1

Page xi constitutes an extension of this copyright page.

LIBRARY OF CONGRESS CATALOGING-IN-PUBLICATION DATA
Ras, Barbara.
One hidden stuff / Barbara Ras.
p. cm.—(Penguin poets)
ISBN 0 14 30.3785 4
I. Title.
PS3568.A637O54 2006
811'.54—dc22 2006043280

Printed in the United States of America
Set in Dante MT
Designed by Elke Sigal

For Anna

Everything in Nature contains all the powers of Nature. Everything is made of one hidden stuff.

RALPH WALDO EMERSON

Acknowledgments

Thanks to the editors of the following magazines for the first publication of these poems, some in different versions and occasionally with other titles:

Bat City Review, "Pursuit"

Cincinnati Review, "El Año Viejo"

Five Points, "Paddling in the Dark"

Georgia Review, "History," "Where I Go When I'm Out of My Mind," "Rhapsody Today," "Ghost Weather," "What It Was Like," and "Big Bull and Little Dog"

Green Mountains Review, "Dream Kisses"

Gulf Coast, "A Wife Explains Why She Likes Country," "Flora," and "Moonshine"

The Journal, "Moving with Children"

Marlboro Review, "Burning"

Massachusetts Review, "Fire" and "Wild Blue Yonder"

The New Yorker, "Our Flowers"

Poetry International, "Happiness" and "Fire and Shadow"

Pool, "The Warmth of the Gulf Stream"

Portland Magazine, "Song"

Shenandoah, "Damage"

Smartish Pace, "Gardens"

Southern Review, "Dogs"

Tex!, "Late Summer Night" and "Secret Lives"

TriQuarterly, "No One Argued About What to Call the Birds"

Wilderness, "Night"

"Texas Sky" first appeared in Between Heaven and Texas. Photos by Wyman Meinzer. Poems selected by Naomi Shihab Nye (University of Texas Press in 2006).

Contents

Part III

Part IV

One Hidden Stuff

Part 1

Rhapsody Today

Maybe today will be the day you wake and for the first time
watch the full moon set surprisingly red over the fine edge of the earth.
Maybe today you'll see the fawn on its gawky legs, the spots on its side
floating tentatively like some leftover dazed grace,
so that you think about animals, their paths to righteousness,
and maybe you'll remember the day a dragonfly rode your shirt front
all the way around the lake, its jeweled body breathless but pulsing,
a little like first love. Maybe today
you'll find gardenias floating in a blue wood-fired bowl and their scent
will bloom into the room like ghostly elephants, bugling softly,
and finally, you'll buy the tickets to Zanzibar,
somewhere with slow fans and ceremonious walking,
where the post office behind the soccer field will smell of cinnamon,
and on the way to the coast you'll visit a village
and the king there will remind you "without evil there is no good."
And though of course evil will enter into every day,
maybe today it will be impersonal, butting into your life quietly
like the deer heads on the walls of the barbecue shack, or insidious
but distant like the human ear in a lab somewhere growing on the back of a mouse.
Maybe you can put even these out of your mind along with the cruelty
of strangers and imagine that today's the day a little bit of time
might stop, suspended in the foot a great blue heron holds above the water,
or maybe you'll watch the mourning doves and discover they warble
as they fly, so eternally amazed by flight that they call, *I'm doing it, I'm doing it.*
Why not make today the day you look
at the back of your eyelids in a fresh way, the glitter there
reminding you of the beach, the starstruck sand you sifted as a child,
sometimes finding a shell the size of a large speck and wondering
about the sound of the sea held in its infinitely small swirl
and what kind of ear it would take to hear it.

By now maybe it is noon, the sun squandering itself
like a coin burning a hole in the blue pocket of sky,
and you think of the hours in the dead of the day in a dusty square,
a colonial city somewhere in Boyacá, and you remember
a burro in a plaza the size of a classroom, you waiting for the bus,
the burro waiting for nothing, while a dust devil picked up spinning, wind and dirt
dancing quietly, and you told yourself *Remember this*, the burro, the dust, and you
wrapped in a drenching solitude, and after all these years, you do.
Maybe today you'll make another memory like that, maybe it'll be the pelicans
and their orderly untalkative lineup in the sky with wings practicing
the language of knives. Maybe it'll be the man shrimping,
a silhouette on the horizon at sunset, flinging his circular net up into the air to flash
a dainty daytime fireworks before it sinks into the sea.
Maybe it won't be today, maybe tomorrow, an even better day,
the brassy moon setting as you rise, maybe bouncing a bit before it slips
blissfully into the ocean, the Indian Ocean, of course, and overhead
the fabulous wingspan of new birds, hungry
for the blue horizon.

Remorse the Color
of Lavender

Spiders have surrounded the house with their fall fanfares,
each a lone assassin in its web, spitting out cocoons of eventual spiderlings.
Yesterday on the Loop cow number 6148 went by in a slatted trailer,
her ears standing straight up in the wind as if she were hearing
last instructions to the faithful for you know what.
In my next life I want to be the namer of paint colors—
Loss the color of coffee, Awe the iridescence of goldfish,
Never the color of stars.
        If thought travels at 155 possibly meaningless miles an hour,
how long will it take me to get from my mind to yours,
from red to green, from ontogeny to phylogeny,
all those recapitulations like bad roads over mountains where rivers
start to descend and you pick one and follow it
out into a dry valley until it evaporates, and when the water ends,
you stop as if at the end of a long pilgrimage.
        It takes a nanosecond to get from here
to rage and a lifetime to get from cleanliness to godliness,
though who knows if you'll recognize God
when you arrive: Pyrenees? Gurdjieff? Duckweed?
Maybe the matter is thinking doesn't matter, unless
you are objecting to war, praying for peace, while beautiful new syllables
keep rising up unbidden in your mind:
        Jalalabad, Mazar-e-Sharif, Kandahar,
incantations you repeat until they scare you, like that improbable word
"evildoer" the President keeps using, as if he'd just consulted
a thesaurus.
        And back at the paint factory, I'll be naming Terror
the color of many people, all of us on our knees, begging for our lives.

No One Argued About
What to Call the Birds

A night sky with pain in it poured its dark
over the back door where we stood in the cold
losing each other and all I could think of
were things of no use, which was everything—
the snow squalid at our feet, in the yard
the deserted garden and the deracinated clouds
obscuring the stars, even time mocking our stillness,
its hands sweeping away from each other reluctantly,
then crossing back, again and again, and us forfeiting
that perennial dillydallying, that contact.
What if I had said, Please, come back?
Who will bless the slaughterhouse? Who will mince the garlic
into a mass of perfect diamonds to toss into the salsa?
Who will call the flamingoes?
What if I had said, Stay?
Let me tell you about the photograph of a brain remembering
that looked like the white faces of monkeys we saw together on a coast.
Let me tell you about the sea ducks at Limantour, a pair diving
at the surf line, under and over, always in tandem.
About the small harp I saw in the window
of a music store, how the strings were strung
between a straight edge and a curl of wood, and I thought
about the half step between rapture and rupture.
And let me read you this line from Herbert who wrote,
"The wind understands that to really suffer, one has to be faithful,"
so that we can sit together again and go on and on about grief
until it becomes as bearable and orderly
as a row of pigeons taking up every inch of a roof ridge
all looking the same way in the rain.

Burning

The train is making its 3 a.m. passing, whistling
at the crossings where no mechanical arms keep cars off the tracks.
In minutes another train will repeat the warnings in reverse, wailing
into the night like a woman who's done many things in the dark
and lingers over them with regret. All I want
is a short freefall into sleep, swells and lulls, that insouciant blue.
Of course I miss the ocean.
No one, really, could not love the idea of a small boat at home
in its boathouse by the dock.
On the motorcycle growling down the street, an angry man is leaving
his wife, though he won't know what to say to his friends,
any more than another man could explain the joy of trapping
a marten with a Victor leghold, 1½-single-spring,
or for a farmer to tell how many swallows sleep in the dozen gourds he's hung
from a pole and crossbeams, the birds sliding down the inside curves to bunch up
at the bottom and still at dawn, they wake and fly.
The sheep I summon come too fast to count, every other one a Dolly.
I should get up and write the President, ask why more of anything,
when at our present rate, we're already two planets too few.
The air of our neighborhood is scorched
from the burning of the house across the street, the home of the ferret
we let out of its cage on mornings of our neighbors' vacation and found again
evenings in the scarf drawer, a cozy bedouin in a caravansary.
Should I go outside to kneel in the garden or get up
and read about evolution, our slow stuttering out of urschleim, and wonder
if there's a point at the top of the rise where we'll begin a descent back, unless
this is it.
Who wouldn't feel rootless, the world driven by greed,
though it wasn't money that made me move
miles and miles from the beautiful city by the blue bay.

Swifts spend almost their entire lives on the wing, their nights
awake in endless flight, in pursuit of dreams and bugs.
But why did the black dog run the shoulder of the bypass, plodding
along with the traffic, but looking back at each car, looking back
again and again to ask, Is this it? Is this it?
We have already rescued two dogs, one draped
at my daughter's door like she has slept at all the doors of all our recent houses.
But when I think badly of moving, my mind shudders up the homeless man,
the blanketed one who prowled downtown streets,
barefoot, in rags stiff with dirt, as if he'd just returned
from forty days in the desert.
He'd pull a match from a matchbook and hurl it lighted
at passersby, hissing and hexing our passings as we went home
to the houses already burning in his mind.

In the Face of a Flower

The spiderwebs and their moley egg sacs are still at the window
my daughter offered to wash for forty bucks. Beyond
in the side yard no one mows, pink daisies have sprung up,
nodding in the breeze, their still centers anchored by hairball roots.
I worry that I won't remember how to enjoy a party.
At the last one I felt like a dog in a field of fireflies,
registering something, nothing, something, nothing.
It was either loneliness or spite that made me eat
the grasshoppers passed around the room.
They tasted stale, the flavor of seeds
retired from making music in very old gourds.
Yesterday lightning came as close to the house
as a crack in a shell comes to a yolk,
and I thought back to my mother saying, "Stay back
from the window," where I wanted to press my face to see the sky split
and let through a little of heaven's light.
In those days there were pussy willows and lilacs,
on TV Crusader Rabbit, more real to me
than the chickens here flattened on the side of the road into cartoon stars.
I want to shake the magnolia tree to see if I'm strong enough
to move any of the darkness inside its tangle of branches.
I want to stare into the face of its white flowers to ask,
Where is the pain petal? Where is the bell petal?
As if together they could explain belonging.
A Polish poet told me that in his country they call the squirrels
Basia, giving me back to my inner nature
and my great-grandfather in Miadzol who cured snakebites
and welcomed the gypsies, letting them camp
where the fields were empty. I once dreamt of their singing,
"Aachie la la, aachie la la," a singing that had the feel of a single butterfly

wafting across a highway to the coast, wandering above cars
the way a pure soul might wander through a voluptuous caravan,
through the smell of wood smoke rising into the hot air,
adding the burning inside trees to the longing the rest of us give up
repeatedly to the heat of the night,
trying to empty ourselves of that deeper what.

Fire and Shadow

In the fawn, its ears like pearly shells, so thin
they let through morning light
as mauve, and in the doe that stares back at you
as if at the long flame of a tall candle flickering in the forest,
and in the lay of an abandoned dress,
layers and layers of taffeta, the kind of garment you'd leave behind
when you wanted to travel light on horseback,
on a horse happiest at the edge of the ocean,
where after a long gallop in the surf's foam, together
you walk, the waves pounding the beach one heartbreak at a time,
and on the journey home, you pass the buzzards on the rail bed,
pass the dark thicket where a rabbit is pulling tufts of wool
from its chest for nesting, you go on, past the farm
where the man from Montana taught you the abracadabra of apples,
starting with the rootstock MM111 and grafting
Northern Spy, Vista Bella, and Splendor onto one tree,
onto one tree!
And you pass all the people who are bedding down,
each in a separate servitude, the lucky ones
who have chosen to slave for joy, even if on bad days
joy is a mean master holding scissors to their heart,
to the hearts of their dogs, and at last you pass
the lake where the geese once rose in a V off the water
and you flattened to make way in the air over you for their flight.
It will be dark by the time you arrive, a contagion in the air,
so you take cognac or maybe the kerosene you bought
in a colder city lit by the blue light of the bay,
and you douse your hands with big, smelly splashings, lighting
a match to watch flames whoof up from your palms
like the hurts of your childhood,
bouquets of furious yellow flowers blooming
in one instant and dying in the next, leaving
what's left of the dance, after the dancer stops.

Shoplifting a Future

At sunset, thin clouds turn into sleek flames tamed to a peachy pink.
I pass perfectly new goats and wonder when my new life
will debut and with what ceremonious christening, everyone with a ribbon
to cut, a shovel to break ground, a magnum of bubbly
to smash on the hull of something hulking, and me
asking what's auspicious about rupture and how long
before my break will break and the future I pursue will appear,
beautifully clear, perhaps in the entrails the guy next to me
at the truckstop is eating,
and for a minute I think, sure, I could make this
an adventure, invite my best friend, even if she hates quests.
Is it the predictability she abhors? The smug knowingness of the hero?
Personally, I'd welcome a sign that good will triumph in the end.
What if the devil is not in the details, but in the cruise control, the black box,
in the booth behind me with some buddies, scanning the scene for chumps,
maybe the man at the counter muttering, "It's too late
to add your name to the list," maybe the two couples arguing
about white folks, whether they smell like wet dogs or dirty sheets,
maybe one of the five presidents discarded in Argentina last week,
or else "That one," a demon says, pointing at me,
"the scared one, trying to steal a future. She may be scared,
but wait till she finds out she's not scared enough."

The Warmth of
the Gulf Stream

My friend is in a classroom teaching Rilke, the way his autumn
winds up and down the clock of the long now. Here at the Holiday Inn
Sinatra is singing about kicks and cocaine, the TV announces a little snow,
and the whoosh of the gas log in the fireplace summons up the heavy breathing
in last night's dream, the wacko who took me hostage
muttering he still had more to learn about being Santa.
No shit, I wanted to say, a guy like you who's probably spent too many years
unbuttoning the dark places in your mind, each month another zipper off the track.
In the bedroom he tied me to a chair, while he slammed clothes
from one side of the closet to another as if expecting to find a disguise,
a way out, finding nothing like the surprise at the back of my grandmother's closet
under the hall stairs—a small door, just right for a five-year-old,
opening into another closet on the west side of the house
my grandmother rented out, always to women, most batty.
How many memories can I stand, crime dreams and childhood, and don't forget
the foxes hanging with my grandmother's clothes, the collar of foxes
she'd wear over suits, even the heads, their pointy snouts and glass eyes
a stunned homage to deceit, frozen things
far from the shabby swirl of leaves in the fall, caught on the air
in a drift or a swoon, the way I wish time would slip and idle, take on
a grander scale, something like the Gulf Stream always off our shores,
unseen currents that you could trust in because they blunted the cold
and made the water swimmable and believe me, whether you swam or not,
it was childhood, it was buoyant.

Moonshine

Out here in the backyard, we're watching the moon to see if it's closer,
brighter, bigger, anything special, being it's the last fullness
on the last solstice at the end of the millennium,
and though it looks the same, it's bathing everything in the kind of light
you notice when you think this is it, the end of something, a glow
you want to inhale, hoping it will make you light-hearted.
Moonlight has turned the sky an adolescent blue,
backlighting the winter trees so they overhang
the yard with black lace. It's turning the rubber factory Tuscan colors
so that it rises over our streets like a castle.
If the moon were fauna, it would be a goat.
If the moon were a tool, it would be the little mirror the dentist uses
to see what's wrong with your teeth. If it were ten thousand small things,
it would be bubbles in champagne, always rising.
Amazing how much the moon can do with borrowed light,
with emptiness, when today all the talk is about money.
If the moon were silver, it would be a gaze ball
in the big garden of space, reflecting the earth in miniature.
If the moon were flora, it would be the spent cup
of a meadow beauty after the bloom is gone.
It's a long way from Tuscany to the neighborhood church
and the marquee that claims "The Saints: God's Handkerchiefs."
If the moon were a pill, maybe it would be God's aspirin.
It's December, but warm enough to be outside without coats. We're trying
and failing to feel the passage of time in the slight breeze,
trying and failing to imagine the next moon filling in the next century.
The pecan trees reach long and languorous toward some hosanna
in the highest, the roots of the oldest set down in the days of the dark enslavement.
Where's the handkerchief, the saint, the God for that?

El Año Viejo

To end the old year, stuff some old clothes full of straw,
no voodoo, no hair from the neighbor dog, no nail clippings
from your spouse. Just straw—
preferably dry and purposeful, like what they laid
on Milan streets to quiet the wagons during Verdi's dying.
Start early so that the Old Year can hang around for a while, perhaps
scaring some birds in the bargain. Before midnight
on New Year's Eve, set fire first to his toes, letting the flames climb
hungry as a goat, surely as a song.
Before you see the old year playing out in the past year's burning,
El Año Viejo gives up scenes from his own past, a far land
you both remember, where the old year burns in every village,
amid misery and guns, drugs and blood, and suddenly you see
the pig's head hung for a raffle in the café where you ate empanadas
when you, too, were among them, on the mountain
with no name among many nameless mountains
rising off the edge of the Valle del Cauca
between tiers of bougainvilleas and mist.
Then the Old Year, full of last straws and bags of wind,
offers up some fresher visions: handcuffs and roses, the loose valve
of your mother's heart, fluttering instead of doing its business,
the skateboard newly arrived in your daughter's life, there with its skater,
flirting with gravity, and as you begin to have second thoughts
about your jeans and once-favorite white shirt on their way to embers,
you feel yourself swept along by loss, so much burning here and away,
so many coffins and even more unburied dead, stars wandering off course,
inescapable destiny—and then BANG! BANG-BANG-BANG-BANG-BANG!
Be glad someone has hidden firecrackers in the pants pockets of the Old Year
to startle you into feeling more alive, the way you resolve to be
now and forever, alert to each moment, cherishing each blade

of the erstwhile grass burning itself into a new year, and while smoke
rises into the surprisingly light night, let go of your pain
a while longer, lose the feeling of being a stranger to your life.
The moon is almost full, and the Old Year is almost ashes.
Throw more wood on the fire and let its glow play
warmly into the wee hours. You don't have to be the last to know,
however late, that while suffering ends, fear lasts forever. Look.
The real work of fire is to eat and to sing.

Dream Kisses

Slender leaves are kissing up to the sky, rustling the trees.
Breezes swing and sway and blow a touch of fever
down every street in your body, fanning your fancy,
a hunger for kisses, for kissing everyone,
because, like mountains, they are there.
Take the dentist—his kiss will be a jaunt to Romania,
or the guy at the gas station; you know he's smarter than he looks
and his kiss will recite the names of all the oil wells in Texas.
Forget life insurance and Palm Pilots. Discover
the someone next door who's a catalog of grasses waiting to happen—
sugarcane, oats, and rye, the many masters of intoxication.
In some kisses you'll taste the history of insincerity,
but don't mistake it for the taste of madder,
the red of old livery and shame, all those writers
you've never read, Novalis, Bakhtin, Catullus,
whose kisses taste like pomegranate and dust.

The average tongue has eight thousand taste buds, packed in
like an armada of ducks waiting to be flushed from a lake.
This year three thousand languages will disappear, dispensing with
countless words for kisses and how to miss them.
But don't capitulate to arithmetic. Move on to the rancher
scorching prickly pears until their needles burn
like birthday candles, and in the whoosh
of the torch beckoning his drought-stricken cattle
you'll hear the past rush back, that night in 1966
under the roller coaster at Lincoln Park after the dance, kissing
the boy with blue eyes and black hair,
all epic magic and smug magnificence, heedless of the grind of time
that would eventually shut down the ballroom, the tunnel of love,
and fling us all into unimaginable futures,

mine, for instance, where I'm now contemplating a slow lean
into the Slovenian poet, whose kiss will praise the mushrooms
in the neat woods of his country.

Whoever thinks this is a poem about sex
should get busy inventing their own kisses,
the kiss that blows the fuse, that digs the grave,
the kiss like an old car you exit only by reaching out the window
to work the door handle from the outside.
Remember never kiss for revenge more than once.
Avoid pratfalls, derring-do, noblesse oblige.

Be sporty. Kiss the Czech golfer
and the Andre Agassi look-alike who sold you flowers.
Forget the self-described explorer, his kiss
will reenact Cook's conquest of the Pacific,
and beware of the man in the brown sweater
on Flight 252 who handed you a pillow, his eyes
as black as the wells where Mayans tossed their sacrificial bodies.

Remember there's more than enough darkness to go around,
and that inside concrete, rebar does its silent work out of sight,
and in this it is like dream kisses,
keeping our walls from falling,
night after lonely night.

Where I Go When I'm Out of My Mind

Leaping out of the barn dance of my brain, where everyone else
can hip-hop, enjoy their murky drinks laced with Ecstasy,
and because that cute blonde in the dark corner with the shirtless guy,
dancing like she wants to smear the tattoos off his chest with her tits,
could be my daughter, I dash off to a middle-ageish bar,
a drink called the Ponce de León, an ungraspably dreamy color,
and that guy who dumped you in college sits down at your table, alas,
he's always loved you, only you, it hit him like the blow of a Zen master
when he saw your masterpiece in the *New Yorker*, your sense of whimsy,
so like Chagall's, wandering lonely as that woman up on the ceiling,
and just when you're sure he's going to lean over and kiss you that kiss you hope
is as fruity as it ever was, he pulls a manuscript out of his briefcase,
800 tattered pages, and you're out of there, but the outside
is looking like that painting by de Chirico, the girl with the hoop
playing alone forever on the haunted street,
and though it's the same painting Lustig made you write about in class
for days in a darkened room, and you wrote and wrote
like some strange tree shedding leaves in the night,
it's just now you see the deserted train, churning up melancholy,
but what you think is melancholy's smell,
is the odor of spent smoke wafting back from the backseat of a car
parked at the tennis courts one junior high-school afternoon,
Alice and Bruce in front, and you kissing the friend of a friend for experience,
that nameless guy with his insistent rancid tongue in your mouth
that felt like the starfish you once carried home in a pail, leaving it to die on the porch
and after a lifetime of looking back, you want to blame your parents
for not teaching you the Tao of catch and release, when it was you all along,
lacking a respect for life, draped as your own life was in the tight satin dress
you bought at Norman's mother's shop, before Norman and you
ruined your friendship by—No, this has got to stop,

where are you Mr. Night, where is Chagall's happy donkey when you need him,
where is that other life, a lucky life, maybe a Stern poem,
where the ecstasy is more real and much safer, or perhaps a little nap,
but in your dreams, you find yourself pulling worms out of your body,
and though you wake thinking you hadn't finished, you move on, trying
to think better thoughts, wishing you could inhabit the blue
inside the red tulip, the starry cross section of a papaya,
the glass vaults of eau-de-vie, operatic arabesques
on the top shelf of the Gotham Grill, one sip of one of those and you could soar,
and why not an eagle, even if it turns out to be the one
at Hampton Beach this August dive-bombing the throngs,
stealing hot dogs, casting its wing shadows over the toddler
looking up now from this bit of darkness for Mommy, who, uh-oh,
has just asked herself if life is going to be a party she was left out of,
a thought driving her out of her mind, anything to escape the teenagers
with the angelic bodies floating thinly that way because
they've been smoking something other than pot, she knows
it's probably spray-painting death on the walls of their hearts,
and though her friend the *philosophe* would say, "God writes death on all our hearts,"
she suspects this is the devil's work, she recognizes the script,
that heavy metal lettering and in fact it was that interminable Metallica song
that made her flee her blanket, desert her kid in search of the perfect tune,
the tiny dancer she knows is shining her tiny headlights
on the full-sized highway, and when she gets there, she'll rethink
all her waywardness, learn that Foucault kind of talk, and stick to the road,
the black macadam stretching ahead like some infallible sentence.

Part II

Song

What if it's really waves, only waves
making their restless peace on the broken shore,
the lull between them like a held breath
before it's blown into air as music.
Haven't I always missed the ocean, the way its salt
buoyed me up inside the wet, the air above warmer than the water below,
the liquid line between breathing and not, so innocent, so permeable.
Floating there, over the deep, untouchable bottom, out past the line
the waves made as they curl to hurl themselves on the sand,
I could be far from the rinky-dink, the hullabaloo, far even
from the headlongingness of water rushing forward
and sloshing back, like desire,
going nowhere.
Over and over the waves break on the gleaming sand
while a gull diving in and out
of the perfect again and again
draws a thread between the air and the water
sewing together their beautiful blues
as if to mend the wound of the world.

Fire

Speaks in the bush of God up there in the desert mountains, plaintive
perhaps, calling from a safe distance like a kid on the sidewalk,
calling you out to play. At night fires sing
between villages, in little arias on the hillsides, they sing brightly so a man
watching the dark through the window of a bus hears them and understands
bad faith and vows to give back the shovel he stole from the butcher,
vows never to slaughter the pig and to feed it the cherries it loves from his hand,
and the young woman beside the man on the bus seeing the same fires
realizes she has come so far from home that the only prayer she can pray
must be spoken in tongues, because they share the shape of flames, and at the end
of the most wordless prayers she prays she will see the little bird again, the one
with the feathers the yellow of the guayacán, the yellow
of the candles that lit the house with the blue roof where Lalo and Fernando
played guitars and sang their heartbreak into the dusky vaulted rooms.
The voice of fire hums in the fields where old grass passes it blade to blade
like the sorrowing of a whole neighborhood over the death of a beloved dog,
and when it is done burning the voice of fire smokes low in the sooty field
that will in time grow greener, green enough for a dance.
Fire smolders in dormant volcanoes and sleeping teenagers
and when the fireflies begin to rouse and appear
high in the crowns of the loblollies, one evening, a mother, who was once
humbled by the fires she saw on the road to Ipiales, hears the voice of fire
calling softly on a summer night, she goes out
to see the comet make its now nightly whisper across the sky, and she walks alone
down to the lake and swims
out to where the comet's smear of light reflects on the water,
she swims out to touch the icy fire made warm on the black sheen of lake.

Happiness

As in the slow breath of the dog on its side, stretched out,
its legs raised a bit so that all fours touch the wall, each paw
making happy shivers like the shudders you felt this morning
driving the kids to school, down the sinewy road past the field
where the grass in the low light though the fall air
had the merest hint of silver and swayed, toward you, then away.
Sometimes the voice of happiness hides up the sleeves
of your husband's shirts, laughing softly in the drawers under the bed,
and often it comes from elsewhere, that place in the distance
where light starts out to deliver its cargo, proving
that everything you see is in the past.
Sometimes the voice of happiness dances, skipping to folk tunes that hold
the animals of your country, and you dance, too, to feel their fur,
their cousin skin, their something else feathers.
The voice of happiness will tell you
it wants to write everywhere, in the tattoos of teenagers,
on the lintel above the door where the priest wrote the blessing
on Epiphany, and once in prison,
when there was nothing else, the voice of happiness took the prisoner's hand
and together they wrote on empty cement bags so that when they were done,
their letter weighed many pounds.
The voice of happiness can sleep for weeks,
and then wake suddenly to say, "Hold on
to the way the arms that inhabit the shirtsleeves want to hold you,"
and then speak in your daughter's voice when she says,
"Put your mouth closer to the phone so I can smell what you're eating."
And at the end of the day, when the dog
is outside licking the glass of the porch door, pausing for long moments
with her tongue on the window, in her eyes the voice of happiness
begins begging,
the way you want happiness to begin every conversation,
with three quick chaste words, "Let me in."

Dogs

Across the street, chained to the back porch and intent on barking
the crowns off my front teeth, a black pit bull is practicing
take me take me take me take me,
he knows his human is leaving any day now
for the coast, a trip to Big Sur, he said, to pick up some rocks,
and the pit bull is ready, every short hair ready to ride in the passenger seat
of the white Cadillac with shark fins and big windows,
he's ready to hang his head out and let the wind blow into his open mouth,
blow that running sensation all the way down into his pit,
where his little bullish soul is charging at red flags
all the way to California, as far
as its silver chain will allow.

Kitty-corner from my house a dog is staked out to guard an abandoned carcass
of a place. No one comes, no one goes, and yet the house keeps filling,
the work of some wild turkey whose dream of ownership
took a turn toward the dark side and set to saving junk,
junk flotsam, junk jetsam, banjo junk, jukebox junk, spare tires, spare time,
spare aprons from the abattoir, spare parts
that have lived alone so long they've forgotten their names.
And the dog there, barking like the kind of boss
that paces the office with black moods, his jeans drooping
so low you can see the top of his butt crack
and you have to look away.

Down a ways in the yard of the shotgun shack next to the water tower,
there's an old mutt that wails. Each time he starts up as if he's going to enter
infinity, as if this time his breath will hold, his voice will go on forever
and he'll croon himself out of being just a mutt among the many on Nantahala,
forget the time he got so close—for God's sake he was practically a shoo-in
for the role of Tramp—until he got to the spaghetti scene and blew it
when he bit Lady in the neck.

The voices of dogs—they can pierce every armor in the day,
penetrate the deepest thoughts no matter how mummified,
because on good days the voices of dogs fly like arrows
coated with the pure poison of desire,
and on bad days, they are lances from the heartwood of plane trees
dipped in the despair that collects under the sheet of ice
on the water bowl by moonlight.

I barely but do remember the ice man stopping in front of the Earle Street house,
his wagon pulled by a horse with demonic black blinders.
Shovel in hand, my grandmother would race Mrs. Kowalsky out
to scoop up the horse droppings for her rosebushes.
What did I care about rosebushes, manure, a kid like me still eating ants,
domesticating the old chicken coop we called the hutch-a-hutch?

Maybe it's okay I ended up here, an old neighborhood, hundred-year-old pecans
soaring above the rooftops, the dogs
keeping things humble, my own dear doggie in the yard, demurely barking
in in in, undespairing, patient little queries,
barking not for nothing, not like that sonofabitch
down the street with the high-pitched yapping, an overgrown cricket, really,
I know I know I know—I know, I know, I know,
her humans inside behind the heavy curtains, ignoring her,
a retired dentist and his wife. I bet he brought the green
dental chairs home after he closed his practice, and they're both facing the television,
I bet they're watching the reruns of *Dragnet, The Price Is Right,* turned up
so loud the plastic grapes on the TV are vibrating.

Could I ever forgive Mrs. Adams in tenth grade for reprimanding
me in front of the class for reading *Catcher in the Rye*,
thus teaching me all I needed to know about authority.
I wonder if she's dead now, if she's come back in the body of Ruby,
the black-lab-and-collie mix with the saber tail.
There on Nacoochee, halfway between the rubber factory
and the chicken plant, Ruby's brain is stalled, her voice, low
and weary, letting out a slow *I dunno, I dunno,*
her sense of smell addled by the voodoo mix of rubber
with a galaxy of chicken parts.

This is my company, the voices of dogs, abandoned dogs, shunned dogs,
dogs that have never seen the inside of a church,
bewildered songsters, barking lunatics, visionary mongrels,
singing till they bark themselves raw or divine.

What would Jesus do?
He'd start by getting down on the ground, he'd start by wrestling the dogs
in the dirt and letting them pin him, letting them win and lick his face
and take on important airs, like dragons.
Then he would let them off their chains,
their stakes, their measly allotments of ropes,
and Pit Bull would finally roam up to Beulah, where the lost souls
sit in front of the crystal shop, and he would lay his nose on a foot
and let the Wild West smell of a boot mingle
with the chaos theory of the sidewalk.

Junk Dog would run up to the old house that's been boarded up,
and nose around, maybe get inside to an emptiness so pure he can whiff up
the recent bats, their long fingers draped with the skin of wings, sniff
up their comings and goings, all the details
down to their little clutchy toes.

Dentist Dog would run up to the Civil War Store on Satula
and hang around there a long time, quietly trying to figure out
the gray and the blue of it, until Wailing Dog came up and they would reenact
the spaghetti scene until they got it right.

Ruby would make her way to the Gold Kist plant and spread out
under a truckload of chickens in a holding bay, where cooling fans
keep the birds crated a dozen stories high
from dropping dead in the heat before they can kill them.

And me, I would roll around in silence, I'd get lost in reveries
of the buttonwoods in the winter park where the duck pond froze over
and I skated with my mother in her long green coat over a vast ice world
flavored with wool. I'd go back to the feeling in the apple tree
in the side yard where I'd climb to the third tier of limbs
and feel so possessed by solitude, it was a perfect Bazooka bubble,
floating me away from the nausea of the school bus, away
from Milton, the dumbshit driver, who never even tried to stop
the kids from taunting me, and I will go back to the dogwood
below the bedroom of my childhood, and watch it unfold its papery blossoms
like origami, like fragile pink tickets.

And when the train goes by at five o'clock, freighted with the ten thousand desires
for the ten thousand things we hope will deliver us
into the out-of-body experiences we long to disappear into
and return from, changed, at last, truly charitable,
I'll say good-bye to Pit Bull and Ruby, farewell to the dogs
searching out new neighborhoods to serenade,
I'll let the train whistle whistle away
all my failed ecstasies, all my perfect pains,
and I'll tilt my head back and howl.

Pursuit

When I left, I went to find the white peach blossoms
in a distant province, I waited there in an orchard until the flowers fell
and drifted from the branches like memories of waltzing with mama
under the arbor, and while I watched, a petal stuck to the black nose
of the farmer's sleeping dog and then I moved on.
I went to a market where there were red mountains
of tomatoes, busheled pools of jasmine rice,
feathery piles of cilantro, its smell like a mysterious cross
between medicine and dirt, hunting and gathering.
I bought yellow flowers in a jar and brought them back
to the inn where a painter from China unrolled his canvases,
Mountains of the North, Sunlight of the West, and told me
pilgrims in search of beauty must go to Echo Temple,
and there find the monk who keeps the portal to the garden
of mist and rock.

In the morning I left. It was the summer solstice,
and I traveled long in the long light, through many villages with many families.
I passed a family on the plateau, I passed a family tilling highland barley,
their promise of pearly grain in the harvest reminded me
of my grandmother, the single pearl drop she
gave me from her secret mirrored box, and how she always arranged
grand meetings at the harbor, big picnics in the woods
where all the women wore satin ribbons in their hair.
Towards evening, I passed a family herding at dusk,
cows with shaggy coats looking back longingly at the shine
of the lake in the valley, its blue the color of bell music and the lost ring
I found at the end of winter in the waning snow.

So many families in one day and the cows' thirst
made me homesick, and I began to tire of the road, lonely lunches
under pretty trees, always the elusive horizon, its beautiful stretch
like cellophane where it meets the sky.

And so, my love, I am back.
Let's open the window to let in the fresh air
and the sound of the horse dancing and snorting.
Let's dine on delicious crabs and fragrant liquor.
Sing me again your songs about the land here,
its golden mountains, silver soil.

Flora

Isn't it a joy to look up from your book
and see the slow fire of pink taking hold
of the trees' crowns across the street?
Clouds of rouge float and burst at once
into spring. Trees are dreaming of bees and banquets,
hosting sorrows too precious to hide.
Is it blasphemy to think of petals
as the lips of God, the tongues of God
asking, "Is it all right? Is it enough to live and fall
in love and die in view of this beauty?"
Thousands of flowers, even more petals, reckless
in their thirst for the old rain in deep dirt,
ruthless in their hunger to hold on. "Look
at how still we can be even without a mirror!"
Until at last they all ravish the ground.

Ivy is entering the bedroom through a window crack,
tickling the space with shoots of green. At first
poignant in their exploration of air, tendrils, desperate
with nothing to cling to, curl themselves
into corkscrews before finally finding
the wood to clutch for climbing.
In no time the entire window is alive in ivy, ignoring
the separate realms of outside and in,
while behind the house, bamboo frames another space.
At night you can hear it growing—
"Enough rancor! Enough betrayal!"—
its green explodes with sweet vulgarity,
deftly shaping a bamboo parlor.

Clouds

It's an afternoon of blue skies, white clouds, big dollops of coconut mousse,
as if some giant kept dishing it out like there was no tomorrow.
On a day like today, you'd expect the clouds to sing, the voice of
John Lennon, Harry Belafonte, predictably God, humming absently
in his chummy, rummage-around-in the-refrigerator tone,
a guy you could ask your most burning questions, starting with the big bang
and working backwards, ending with the edge of space, and then what?
But so far, silence—a busy day for a deity with so many solicitations,
the complaints with fluffy white frosting people try to pass off
as prayer.

Beneath it all I'm driving east
with a friend from the desert, talking
the way women do, about the arithmetic of love,
its pluses, minuses, long marriages dividing,
the geometry of grief, new sides to familiar triangles.
If you have four people, add one, and take away two,
how many are left, and which ones are crying?

It's a long drive, and my friend and I want to just oooh and aaah
over the magnificently obsessed whipped cream
in the sky like lost thoughts, vows of chastity, 20,000-foot
miracles of water and light.
But the clouds have started to pile vertically
into the kind of billowings that could only be called atomic,
and once that's thought, suddenly
there's Oppenheimer, at the first test at Jornada del Muerto
(del MUERTO? you want to scream), admitting
as he did then, *Science has known sin.*
And now, of course, the legacy
of the clouds, *the bomb and its quick and slow armageddons,*

begins to reverberate everywhere and I imagine my friend
thinking about her home in the Great Basin, where poisons
from all the tests in the middle of somebody else's idea of nowhere
tend to pool.

I want to leave this line of thought, let the beautiful clouds
and the trees they marry prove the intelligence of the cosmos.
I want to think about art, the painting of the newborn saint,
who stood in front of the bed where his mother was passed out, maybe dead,
a tiny expert in a ring of light talking a blue streak
at all the servants on their knees, with no one
paying attention to the three dogs in the shadows eating bread.

I wonder how many sheep these clouds could hide, how many
shepherds, and then another voice jerks me back, a male voice
from above. *This*, he says, *has been the death of a beautiful subject*,
speaking of physics,
and now that we've gotten out of the car to stretch our legs,
we begin to hear music, sweetly earnest bells, playing a hit
from the dreamland of the fifties, the standard number
for the last dance now coming improbably from a church,
echoing all the tests and all the sands,
Goodnight, Irene, Goodnight.

Night

The wind came up and I woke on the deck where the blue tarp
put down under my sleeping bag against the guano
of the swallows nesting under the lip of the roof
started flapping wildly, clapping because the wind
had come over the backs of horses, it had come
through armadas of sails and armies of hands,
it had come sledding off the steppes, skidding
off the edges of Extremadura, it had come
through granite and longleaf pines, suddenly supple,
bending in the push and pull of the wind's wooing, blowing
this way and that, intoxicating tree trunks and branches with ideas like lotion.
For a long time, the wind rushed back and forth in locomotives, in chases,
in unrequited love so mysterious it was hard to tell
who loved, who held back, the sudden texture in the air thick
as the mind that was elsewhere until a smile yanked it clear across the room.
Awake, I was hopelessly awake, with the wind inciting the blue tarp
to preposterous blusterings and the wind chimes to mintier mawkish notes.
If only there was a phone, if only it would ring
with an invitation to discuss enlightenment, whether it happens
like three small sneezes in a row or like the endings in Mahler, the music
rising and falling so long you've stopped expecting the last gasp.
And yet, above it all, the wind went on with its swanky rapture, its rapids,
it went on being the pall, the blush, the shudder of sky,
it went on repatriating small skull bones and carrying
the ghosts of passenger pigeons, their acres and acres of wings
darkening the already dark night, the wind went on turning,
whipping up banked fires, then falling into lulls like the hush of adolescents
serious about suicide.

History

Of course wars, of course lice, of course limbs on opposing sides
to remind a body about ambivalence, of course orphans and empty beds and eyes
exiled for blinking in the harsh light. Of course Khrushchev gave Crimea
to the Ukraine in a blind drunk, and yes, land mines and burning skin
and of course organs, some members dismembered
to shake at strangers and their evil, and there is no way
to imagine that a man shaking a dried penis would ever utter the word *darling*.
Of course personal, add starch for pain, add bluing, of course hang
the laundry in the basement, there are thieves in the backyard, of course
departing trains, carload after carload of sorrow,
the man on top of a boxcar waving,
his rifle silhouetted against the white sky, its color draining
the way warmth left the Bosnian after he'd burned the last page of the last book,
knowing he had reached the end of something though it was not end enough.
Of course kisses, the stages of kissing like running borders,
endless conversations, stations of the cross, till even the promise of kissing bores you,
of course teeth gnashing, ethnic cleansing. The cynical will shrug off the past,
the future, the whole left hip of Ecuador slashed for six days of oil,
of course an X on the coats of the sick so they would stand apart
for deportation, of course rogue tumors over the body politic,
the same bodies that took Egyptian mummies and powdered them
to use as food seasoning, bon vivant cannibalism,
and yes civilized men tossed living penguins into furnaces to fuel their ships.
Of course partitions so that after the new territories were defined,
families had to line up on a cliff with bullhorns
to talk to their people on the other side,
of course courage, at times a weapon against yearning, surrender another,
a mother of course goes on setting the table, even if it's with broken plates,
and a friend will say gently of course I want to ride with you to the funeral,

of course of course of course of course,
now then, negotiations, whatever,
palisades, the end of whimsy,
but then one evening though it is wartime,
a man climbs the hill to an amphitheater to play his cello at twilight
and history stops talking for a moment and sighs
while the melancholy of Albinoni
passes from heart to heart and each lifts a little,
the way passing a baby around a room can be sacramental,
and the memories of simple pleasures become more beautiful, the memory
of your joy on a highway to see in the next lane in a neighboring car
a clown take off his nose at the end of the day, the memory
of how your mother laid roses, sweetheart roses, on the cold grate of the fireplace,
and the sudden rain one afternoon in fall after you'd hiked far into the dells
and you huddled deep in your overcoat in the wet,
waiting out the storm with a sheep
that had come up to lean against your side
like a rock.

Part III

Neither Here Nor There

Purple rose up the length of the trees, at first sweet
as if their roots had been dipped in altar wine, then higher,
like doubt rising, belly up.
The light ahead leaden, we drove away from the sun
playing orange trombones across the horizon behind us,
creating the kind of contrast, forward, back, that makes you wonder
about strength, whether there's more fortitude in steeling yourself
for the dark ahead, all that metallic light like irony,
the avant-garde, the night at the end of a lighted tunnel
taking the road under a mountain until the tricky way your mind
clicks and you're in a hole heading down into the deepest earth,
thinking if you were a better person you could manage perspective,
control passion, but what about all that papaya light behind
in the magnificent sky, the rearview mirror blazing like a brick
of fire, something you could hold safely in your hand,
if you could only stop hurting the ones you love.
Maybe it is the sunside of the trees that makes the happiest music,
but could we tell the future from the thickening huddle of trees
ahead, or would we need an animal, the marks it might make
in a clearing while it danced. Believe me,
a certain slant of the wind can lift
even the heaviest heart, but can you imagine
how animals remember, even butterflies with their unlikely
architecture, beautiful armature dusted with beautiful powder,
all for carrying a boneless body, its so-called brain
smaller than its salivary gland and still
their daily dallying and long yearly flights stagger us big brains
sitting here wondering how to balance our minds, find peace
in the present, looking back, peering ahead, wondering
how much of an animal life is lived in its tail,
how much in its tongue.

Paddling in the Dark

The stillness of the lake contains us in our red canoe
in the defined basin of its waters.
It's fall. We have harvested nothing I can name.
Moonshine lies on the water like bombazine
unrolled under an Indonesian sun. We can believe this
because physics and religion have taught us to believe light speed,
transubstantiation. So far, no one has pinned down will.

Vapor hangs like smoky remnants of thoughts, ethereal ruin of desire,
the desire of the lake to be air, the desire of the sky to be water,
the desire of my mind to be still and harmless.
If I have come to the water to be quiet, why
do I keep jumping ship to wander down various roads,
some of them stopping at the kind of inn that in the last century
slept four or five same-sex strangers to a bed.

Coyotes start up a binge of yapping, arguing about death,
whether it tastes more like steak or neck bones.
I wonder how many things that can kill you are also invisible.
We paddle for long stretches without talking. Finally
beavers break the silence and thwack their fleshy tennis rackets on the water,
furry Zen masters practicing the one Zen hand we all long for.
I can't imagine death, the lake more like sleep or loss,
like a place purposefully flooded where a villager
in a black slicker goes out in a boat to find the family farm,
maybe a beloved barn buried under fathoms of water.
Somewhere beneath us in the lake there may be oxygen atoms
that you and I have breathed,
that we may breathe again, with or without wanting to.

Who knows about will, the ebb and flow of control, like our desultory
paddling against lake currents, sometimes against each other.
We don't make much of a wave, only wrinkling the skin of water
that smooths quietly in our wake.
Either the vapor is the lake rising into air or the sky descending into water.

We paddle languidly, nothing in the dark to hurt us, the future
circumscribed by the lip of the lake, the earthy edge a sadness
we can choose to pass at a perfect speed,
slow enough to savor,
quick enough to leave for good,
while the moon keeps spilling itself on the water,
wave upon wave,
and the distance—heartbreaking—
that its light has traveled to become liquid.

Moving with Children

Should you prepare them for homesickness?
Tell them that it's like standing
in a room hung with slabs of darkening meat?
That it is like a skid?
That it is like a question you have to repeat over
and over to people shouting back, "Milk! Milk!"
That it is like chicken pox itching and after it the scabs
leaving shallow empty puddles in skin.
That it is like languor slowed down to stupor.
That it is like the train whistle at bedtime
closer now than it's ever been.
"No, not the beautiful melancholy whistling of the train,"
the oldest will say, "Like dump trucks."

In the new land your children will hide.
They will come out of their rooms from behind closed doors,
their eyes red, their shoulders hunched so deeply
they look like they could meet in the middle, the body
folding into itself on the center line.
And when you try to hold them, they jerk,
even the youngest,
jerks away.

Their homesickness will be your homesickness.
Their pain will leap geometrically from them to you.
Their mauve, your maroon. Their spill,
your storm. Their hunger, your begging.
Their cut, your blood. Your blood,
their blood, so they put on blankness like a bandage.

Then maybe one day the cat will run away
and come back to his new home to purr again
in the laps of your children.
You will begin to understand the radio, the broadcaster
who tells of residents in another city who wearied of potholes
in their streets and filled them with mattresses.
Your middle child will say, "I'm glad
I don't live there."

Months later, one Sunday, your children will bring you breakfast
in bed. It will come served on a cutting board
covered with a dish towel because no one could find a tray.
Cold eggs. Warm orange juice.
There will be a little vase with a few small daisies.
Your kids will eat on the floor at the foot of your bed,
all three, not fighting.
Afterwards, you will read to them about a Vermont farmer
who carried deer mice home in a glove.
And though your children will think the girls who got the mice
are happier than they will ever be,
you can see how this thought registers on their faces,
like all things, relative, and for a moment
you will see that they are happy too,
happy enough.

Damage

Hard to tell in this abandonment what was what—
or why they'd need hydropower deep in these woods,
but there's the dam, a wobbly wall of boards bent and broken
by the water's push, its rush to be anywhere but here,
in that, like the teenagers we've brought with us with our talk,
those distant ones we feel closest to when they're somewhere else.
At the stream's edge some still pools
have frozen into pale awkward cakes. The hurt
color of the ice calls to the sun, but the sun
does not come out. The sky's haze goes on forever.
There doesn't have to be a beginning, not of the moment,
not of the place in the path where we began to feel lost,
not of our own time when as young girls we too turned toward meanness
and deceit, and it came to us
so naturally.

The air smells like nothing, or maybe nothing laced
with the dim memory of fecundity leaking
out of the cold core of all the leafless trees.
Splintered pieces of wood angle out from the dam's ruins,
maybe part of the same tree
that marked a death on the highway with a flimsy cross
and next to it, the pink hemisphere of paper flowers
like a gigantic mai tai parasol that made even death look romantic.
If we could choose for them,
would we pick joie de vivre or safety?

To get here we cut through a cemetery, past a new grave
festooned with a rot of flowers, the unrot of plastic floral baskets.
Wouldn't you rather animals gnawing on your bones,
sagebrush carrying away tufts of your hair, or in the absence of sagebrush, rats?
My daughter once announced, Without the legs of ants, everything would fall apart.
Not much later she showed me a photograph of a friend of a friend
with a car battery suspended from rings in his nipples.
I felt old and missed the girl who shopped for flowers
for her dad and said, Not white, white is too formal.

Now, leaving the woods, we cross a meadow topped off
with a demi-glace of sun, a dash of snow,
together casting an icy glow
the color of the Sancerre we drank last night
made from grapes grown on a particular bank of a river,
in a particular bath of light, in a country, far away, where they laugh noisily
when they say *We never thought to rise*
above suffering.

And I wonder how they sink into their own visions of loss, when their kids
go out at night, and you say, "But remember, so few drive, over there,"
reminding me of my daughter's hands on the wheel
as she backed down the driveway, the steely glint
of the streetlight catching her braces, and I think how quickly
we have come to this
and the folly of building a wooden wall against water,
how the stream stalled at the dam's edge, as if to mirror
for a moment the sky's pain, before pouring through the ruins,
reckless and radiant.

Gardens

I don't know if it was the light or solitude or the two together, the butter
and the knife, but when I saw the apron of petals beneath the jobo tree
that the bougainvillea had grown into as if to explore roundness,
I felt the time alone long enough surround me like the dark emptiness
of a deserted playground at night.

Longitude should be the noun for *longing*.

This is where the New World began—Hispaniola, the land
the Admiral of the Ocean Sea claimed
when he carried glass beads, hawksbells, bright buckles, and the word
conquest into the West.

I made a deal with the lizards. They get the ceilings and the walls,
we share the floor, I get the bed.
When I told a gardener that a green one kept breaking our pact
and popping up under the sheets, he told me not to worry,
"He's a clean bird."

Tomorrow would have been my grandmother's hundredth birthday.
I count the years since her death by your age, nearly fourteen,
and I can still see the exact hazel of her eyes, the way she held
her hands together on the table as if in that little temple she could rest
all her weariness, all its weight.
Anna. Your namesake, a word that belongs
with vouchsafe and bosom.

I found your "Lines for Mom" in my notebook—
A forlorn shadow cast upon the sea.

Yesterday I snorkeled out to the far reef, afraid to swim out alone,
but more afraid to tell you that I hadn't done it.
White goatfish, fairy basslets, shy hamlets, and the translucent fish
I couldn't match with a name that had the color of sunstruck sand
and shimmered toward the edge of disappearing,
the way I can almost hear my grandmother's voice
until I reach for it—

Falling, all night long—leaves of mango, leaves of avocado, pink petals
of amapola, the orange flames of the flamboyantes,
all night the botanical world falls, and all day,
the gardeners rake and sweep leaves off the grass,
off the gardens, off cobblestones laid here by Dominican hands
with what dream of what ownership, they sweep
the parking lot where the tourists arrive in cars, in buses, the plaza
where a young black man sweeps bougainvillea petals with a straw broom
as scraggly as bird feet.

Coming back to Spanish, I thought I'd return by the *malecón*, a promenade
by the sea, built over the sands that know their sandness though not the shape
they'll take when the ocean and wind work their interminable work.
Instead I've come by the river to a village in the highlands,
where at night, yellow lights inside iron lanterns
make pools of honey.

Riqueza rhymes with *pobreza*,
but the distance between them marks the ugly lengths greed will go to.
It is noon. Outside my window
the gardeners are laughing.

Cassen Garda, she called it, Cassen Garda,
when my grandmother talked about her arrival in America.
Orphaned, pregnant, and passing through Castle Garden's admitting area,
at eighteen she left behind the best she would ever speak in any language.

The sun creeping up like a spider, you wrote.

Twenty days here and tonight I noticed the ceiling of my room is pink,
and I think of you saying, "Remember
when we all rode together in the morning
and the car smelled of coffee and Oil of Olay?"

Riqueza, pobreza, belleza,
Diego, the head of security in apartment 3,
writes poems and greets me, "Bella!" he says,
only "Bella."

The air is full of butterflies, they wander
into the house, once a yellow one resting
on the framed picture of the wild rose, its wings
clapping ever so quietly. Last night
in a restaurant a black one the size of a small prayer book
landed on Fernando's face and batted its wings
like they were pages flipping to find the right prayer.

Arms raised as people warned . . .
written on your page and crossed out.

Beneath you I wrote: *the dirt here*
is for people who believe in it.

A black lizard with a glaze of blue on its head
came to my balcony, looked at me, and blew a green bubble
with its throat.

As she got older, every time my grandmother bought a new dress
she would say, "I want to be buried in this,"
buying for death what she couldn't give herself
in life.

This morning petals raked from their beautiful lingering under trees
into little piles, small volcanoes of orange, neat mounds of white, lovely breasts of pink,
swept up, but left on the grass, left
like a separate truce, a temporary balance
between suffering and comfort.

An Opera of Blue

Light fell through the trees like lances, like young green lizards
poised on the edge of yellow, breathing with their whole bodies.
Songbirds sang unseen in every one of a row of dogwoods,
and the sky shone a light opera of blue
in a day when the world could be fearless,
choose love, a day that made me want everything inside,
the way I once held my daughter pulsing in my body.

On my way into town, I saw my husband
walking ahead on my side of the street. Traffic was slow.
The little boyishness of his hurrying spun the wheels of my heart.
In one hand he carried a cup, a bag in the other,
two simple containers containing, I thought, the range of marital possibilities.
When we converged at the corner, he leaned into the open window of the car
like a prophetic soul of the inner world and offered me
a delicately fizzing drink.

A Wife Explains Why She Likes Country

Because those cows in the bottomland are black and white, colors
anyone can understand, even against the green
of the grass, where they glide like yes and no, nothing in between,
because in country, heartache has nowhere to hide,
it's the Church of Abundant Life, the Alamo,
the hubbub of the hoi polloi, the parallel lines of rail fences,
because I like rodeos more than I like golf,
because there's something about the sound of mealworms and
leeches and the dream of a double-wide
that reminds me this is America, because of the simple pleasure
of a last chance, because sometimes whiskey
tastes better than wine, because hauling hogs on the road
is as good as it gets when the big bodies are layered like pigs in a cake,
not one layer but two,
because only country has a gun with a full choke and a slide guitar
that melts playing it cool into sweaty surrender in one note,
because in country you can smoke forever and it'll never kill you,
because roadbeds, flatbeds, your bed or mine,
because the package store is right across from the chicken plant
and it sells boiled peanuts, because I'm fixin' to wear boots to the dance
and make my hair bigger, because no smarty-pants, just easy rhymes,
perfect love, because I'm lost deep within myself and the sad songs call me out,
because even you with your superior aesthetic cried
when Tammy Wynette died,
because my people
come from dirt.

Secret Lives

The same moms that smear peanut butter on bread, sometimes tearing
the white center and patching it with a little spit,
the same moms who hold hair back from faces throwing up into bowls
and later sit with their kids at bedtime, never long enough at first,
and then inevitably overtime, grabbing on to a hand
as if they could win out against the pull on the other side,
the world's spin and winds and tides,
all of it in cahoots with sex to pull the kid into another orbit,
these moms will go out, maybe in pairs, sometimes in groups,
and leave their kids with dads and fast food, something greasy
they eat with their fingers, later miniature golf, maybe a movie,
a walk with the dog in the dog park,
where one night a kid sees an old mutt riding in a stroller,
invalid, on its back, its paws up, cute like that, half begging, half swoon,
and this kid, who once told her mom she knew what dads did on poker nights—
"They're guys, they'll just deal the cards and quarrel"—
starts to wonder what moms do out together, whether they talk about their kids,
their little rosebuds, their little night-lights,
or are they talking about their bodies and what they did with them
in Portugal, Hawaii, the coast of France, it's better than cards,
it's anatomy and geography, they're all over the map,
or maybe not talking but dancing—
to oldies? light rock? merengue? Would they dare dance
with *men*, with men in vests? in earmuffs? forget earmuffs!
top hats, younger men in sneakers who catch their eye from across the room.
Now they're singing. Where have they kept the words to so many songs,
storing them up like secrets, hidden candy, the words melting in their mouths,
chocolate, caramels, taffy,
the next thing you know they'll be drinking—or are they already
on to a third bottle, some unaffordable Nebbiolo

from the Piedmont, red wine named after the region's fog
and aging into a hint of truffles.
Soon two of them will walk off together, laughing,
their mouths open too wide, their shoulders, no their whole bodies
shaking, the way a bear would laugh after it ate you,
heartily, remorselessly, they laugh all the way to the bathroom,
where together in the mirrors they try to keep a straight face
so they can put on lipstick the crimson of the sun sinking into the bay.
They blot their red mouths on tissues they toss
over their shoulders, leaving the impressions of their lips behind
on the floor for a tired woman in a gray dress who'll lift them to the trash,
not noticing the moms' lips, not wondering for even a heartbeat
if the kisses there meant hello or good-bye.

The Used Heart

The falling wind plays daftly in the trees,
through the loblollies, the maples, whose alien blooms
she picked off the ground in spring to bring home to water,
and now in summer the slanted, slatternly light
plays through the Japanese pines she loves and worries are dying.

She knows if she said, *Plumbago*,
he would say, *Graphite, what they use*   .
in spark plug wires to carry the charge,
and they might go on to the power of pencils and the current
that flows through all things,
but she shuts it down, closing like a wild cold flower.

In the dimming corners of the room, she sees for the first time
some fire trucks and two chief cars on the floor, set there
in a tableau of pointlessness the man has rescued from his past.
Childhood, something they could talk about but won't, its distant
running like grounded birds, no keel to the breastbone.

The woman wants to admire something, anything.
Night falls. They could be anywhere, a place in the city
she wouldn't park the car, bail bondsmen, pawnshops, desperate
car washes alternating with bars that plastic their storefronts
with silver films of oblivion.

She wants to ask how many pencils it would take
to light up this dark, to describe the unaffordable luxury of loyalty,
its plain forevers, its days of mourning.

Ghost Weather

Now the sky is the color of absinthe.
It's the end of the day. The weather tilts toward thunder, maybe tornadoes.
All the roses have fled, some leaves.
Here and there a hydrangea holds out a still fistful of blue.
The greenish milk of the sky and the faded hush of the flowers
echo maps from when the earth was flatter,
distances greater.

After months of pushing me away, my daughter came into my office
and walked over to my desk to lay her hand on my cheek, wordlessly,
as uncomplicated as birds and sunlight in a garden.
It was after we had moved and our old life was still a dream
we wanted to resume dreaming, and to wake from on a bright Sunday in the fall
to find the neighbors putting together a party, people
walking toward it on the street like magi bearing dishes and bottles.
Her lifelong friends would take my daughter back into the next new
borderline behavior teenagers solemnly cultivate, and while the sun set,
pooling its ripe-pearish light on the bay, the adults would stand around
the grill and watch the salmon smoke and gleam.

Instead I woke to Chechnya, a woman on the front page fleeing
in her bathrobe, in one hand her daughter's, in the other, the girl's teddy bear,
just a mother with her daughter and a toy, running
into the camera, running into the wide eyes of our breakfast tables,
in a bathrobe, a pink bathrobe, for all the Associated Press world to see,
and before the man in Bangor turns to the stock page, and the woman in Duluth
begins clipping coupons, and the homeless guy in San Jose
stops at the newspaper box to shake his head for a moment before shuffling on,
maybe one of us, I hope not a child,
imagines the bombs falling on the fled house,
falling on their pantry, on their shoes, the girl's spelling words, the woman's lipstick
the color of the geraniums by the door that is already going up in flames.

For a time then, my own loss was just as hard to hold as happiness,
and the loss of loss numbed me with the same unworthiness
I felt when an old therapist of mine appeared on TV, a Dutch woman
I'd spent a couple of years with, years back,
now on PBS telling how during the war in occupied Holland she hid Jews,
a father with an infant hidden under the stairs of a country house.
One night the local constable in cahoots with the Nazis came back
to recheck the house, and because the baby was crying and because my therapist
had a gun and no choice, she shot the cop,
and the next day the undertaker hid him in a casket with another corpse,
buried them like that.
I'm glad she saved the family, glad that all the while I lay on her couch,
rehearsing what I now recall as annoyances, the complaints
of a person standing in a swarm of gnats, too stuck to move away from them
into the house, that I never had to picture the two stiffs
stuck together for eternity, face-to-face on their sides, a couple
trying to make the best of an arranged marriage, chatting in bed, comparing notes,
who came to the funeral, who wore black, who ate too many sausages.

Once my daughter woke me out of a fever,
when just the two of us lived in the nearly empty basement
of a brick ranch. She woke me to see if I still inhabited my hot body,
and went back to watching a video on the TV and VCR we bought
from a pawnbroker who said he used to live in Colombia.
I went on sleeping and burning, waking periodically to worry
about my daughter alone in a strange town, the fall hotter
than any of our memories of any weather.

But what about the temperature in Bogotá, a wife on the radio
trying to send news to her husband, missing for months
in a country where kidnappings are so common
there's a weekly broadcast for families to talk to the disappeared,
a sister held on the steamy coast of the Caribbean Sea,
or maybe a cousin in a small city surrounded by mountains planted with coffee
all the way to the top, or maybe a husband in a balmy metropolis in a high valley
crossed by a river, where I lived for a time without knowing
the country would be soaked with blood,
its red rampant, running
as if it had drained from bougainvilleas, ashamed of their beauty,
from cities of tiled roofs, helpless against violence, from the hearts
of several million souls, and to the ones who asked
I couldn't answer why.

And on the radio the engineer begins one of his many rewinds,
pulling back the tape of the woman's voice so that it blurs
like the sound of a fuzzy river, a river running the wrong color,
flowing backwards, so she can try again,
as the radio host assures her is best, try again and again
to keep her voice from breaking, keep it light—
yesterday's *sancocho*, today's soccer, the priest this, the neighbor that—
not too personal, not letting on she's scared he's dead,
that she is missing him,
that we are all missing someone, something,
fugitive gestures we never understood,
the rawness of cut flowers or the monsters
on the terra incognita of old maps, beasts who warn
us about the unknown but say nothing
about the hue of the sky,
the sky that pours itself into us,
and then the thunder.

Part IV

What It Was Like

If they ask what it was like, say it was like the sea
rolling barrels of itself at you in the shadowless light of the shore,
say it was like a spider, black as night, large as a campesino's hand,
a deepness that could balance a small world of dirt as easily as a gift
of gleaming red tomatoes held out to you eight at a time.
If they ask you how it felt, say solitary,
at first the ease of sleeping alone, warm without even a sheet,
then the nonchalance of a dirt road leading down the hill, its dust
raised and re-raised in plumes as each guest departed,
and later, say it was like the blind cat that came out of nowhere
to lie on your tile floor, lifting its face to stare with white marble eyes.
If they ask what you heard, tell them the single note of the watchman,
who coughed his one syllable when you went to bed,
and at the end of every dream when you woke with a simple plea—
stay, go—again, the cough of the watchman.
If they ask about thirst, tell them no one could carry water as far
as it had to go, so that when it was time to rest,
people went to the spigot at the edge of the train tracks
and cupped their hands under the water, lowering their faces to drink.
Tell them a man could stand at noon in the park wearing nothing but underwear
and beg for hours with his cup empty.
Tell them you could sit quietly while phrases you didn't know you knew
rose up in the language there and on an undisturbed lake in your mind
you could back float—that weightless prayer that prays
Let me die with my toes pointing up at the sun.
When they ask what people will eventually get around to asking,
How was the food? Tell them *batata, mamón, guanábana, maní,*
indigenous crops exchanging places with hunger,
giving up to the dark store window whose inventory is one hand
of bananas sold one banana at a time, giving up to little pyramids of limes
by the side of the road and the kids who tend them, dreaming
of a few coins tossed down in the dirt.

Wild Blue Yonder

Perfectly round palmetto trunks roll back and forth in the surf.
Out where the waves break a wild dark tree
stands upright in the ocean, a monument to regrets
too ancient to dissolve in all the water in all the seas.
Some days a young eagle sits in the top tier, preening and staring.

The beach erodes under an onslaught of ocean, an idea I inhabit,
because for people without a homeland,
as Adorno said, reflecting on his own damaged life,
"writing becomes a place to live."
Later the salt air will ache inexplicably in my chest.

In the forest that springs up where the sand ends, cicadas
shriek to their own music, their greedy *gimme gimme*
rises and falls, a tango I like to breathe to,
losing myself in an accordion darkness of dancing and grabbing
a flight to Buenos Aires.

Between the water and the wrack line, tiny shorebirds hop around on one foot,
like knock-knock jokes in search of who's there.
Is trying to be funny a kind of crippled narcissism?
Is that why I'm avoiding the water?
When I look down, the shadow of a dragonfly on the sand

makes me jump, as if I'd said wake me when my lost friend returns
and I felt his hand on my shoulder shaking me
to say it's time to rekindle that weird cynical hope.
Of course it's just a dragonfly, accompanied by an entourage of lovebugs,
pairs stuck together in the after-curse of mating.

For seconds I watch two butterflies swashbuckle toward open ocean
before they disappear like messengers knowing
they will be shot for their bad news, despite their white wings,
their silent beauty.
A battalion of pelicans dislodges holus bolus,

as if the horizon were only a wing beat or two away.
Against the dazzling sky, gulls fly with their stark, parenthetical grace.
Everything is heading out into the blue,
the blue sky that would be blackest space and studded with stars
if not for the air around our round planet, the invisible layer giving us a wrap of
        light.

With such pure blue coming from such perfect clarity,
you'd think we could manage compassion.

Oasis

Out back, the trees with their firm stand and waving limbs
fling out their rooted dread, not at all the escape we were after,
a respite from the miserable president, children killing children,
the Taliban on the old Silk Road bombing
the Buddhas of Bamiyan into dust.
Still the leaves of the trees go on trembling
and the waves the wind makes in the treetops
rustle with the rising and falling sound
that sand makes traveling up and down dunes, whispering,
what we heard in the postcard from a bedouin latitude
where palms floated above the clouds at the horizon,
past an orange oasis where in the dusk, camels stood backlit
by fire, maybe a conflagration big enough to roast several whole goats,
or perhaps many small fires and dust kicking and burning together
in a great dance that could whirl you clear into the afterlife.

A Buddhist monk wrote about the cloud in the paper, yes,
in the very paper you are holding in your veritable hand, touching
the cloud that rained on the forest and the trees and the woodcutter
who sent the wood to the mill that made the sheets they'd call Glatfelter,
Mohawk, nothing about the names of the paper
suggesting Cumulus-over-Maine, Mist-over-Oregon,
Mare's-Tales-over-Alabama, and it means that if I write
a leaf has volunteered to land in my wine,
I am ignoring the cloud in the leaf, the rain in the wine,
the sand in the glass that might have come from the oasis in the photograph,
the oasis I long for—did I tell you about its birds, the twenty-seven birds
flying against the burning sky that has sprouted,
I just noticed, another row of palms, the birds
flying above the camels dying to fold their legs up for the night,
a fine line of birds winging on spectacular wings the size of prayer rugs—
calling me to the oasis I long for,
even though I have always feared the desert.

Texas Sky

The soft air, a big sky, it's easy to imagine being a flower
or that bird with the black-and-white neck bands
under the live oak, life condensing light
into darkly twisting branches.
Nights here produce a bleaker dark,
but on a morning like this, breakfast tacos and a perky tablecloth,
why worry that I'm alone in a new state
where phrases like "shoot from the hip"
take on a new meaning. Why worry
that a person could look up into this openness
and see a speck getting larger and larger as it fell, becoming
the door of a house lifted by a tornado in the next county
and thrown back down here
as if the air were trying to empty its mind,
get rid of things like doors that are never just themselves.
Last night the Perseids streaked the sky with grains of sand
traveling at 137,000 miles an hour and when they flared into our air,
we saw shooting stars. I could disappear in seconds
and no one would notice for a while, flat gone, like the dream
of never moving again exchanged for a city that dreams in Spanish,
one with many tall buildings mirroring the sky,
so that when the wind is up,
big bluffy clouds move in four dimensions
and restlessness feels as natural as vapor
that pauses a moment in front of a looking glass
to look carelessly and move on.

Late Summer Night

A solo trumpet playing Latin music
is blowing the sad heaven
out of the heart of the neighborhood,
dissolving into night like sugar into coffee.
A train passes, hoots, then hoots again,
piercing the dark with many arrows for many hearts,
desires that linger,
then gouge,
and want again.

This morning I woke not knowing where I was or why
there was a jack-a-lope mounted on the hall wall,
dreaming of rabbit time before its antlers sprouted one season
and kept on growing like legends,
as real as you want them to be.
A gray cat jumps on the bed to lay its head in my hand,
its small warmth in my palm like a full-blown rose
brought in from the sun. Summers past
I spent long days fattening on light.
Salt dusting my skin, the sand uneven beneath me,
I was as anchored as I'd ever be.

Now sprawling through a sleepless night,
I count the beats between the curtain's billowing
in and out, as if measuring could defer dread,
but it can't, any more than you can be saved
from wandering by anything but more wandering.
The ceiling fan is churning and re-churning the same air
but it feels hotter, doubling back on itself.
Tonight's a perfect night to rehearse heartache,
how it comes and goes with the breath in the trumpet,

the uncoupling of boxcars, blooms of morning glory
along the fence between the next house and mine.

Of course, flowers don't come back after they've gone,
and it's wrong to call this place mine,
as wrong as the buzzing in my mind, which if I could let it,
would take me back to the bee yard I once stood in
with my friend, the beekeeper, deeply lost
in all the tiny humming and drumming,
like the past and the present praying together,
but instead I think about what they would weigh, all the bees
in all the hives, and how long it would take for each one
to come back from the blossoms
and throw up a little honey or bite you.

Big Bull and Little Dog

The bull's head rides the dining room wall with lonely grace.
Its eyes have a no-directions-needed look
and for black glass balls they concentrate an awful lot of midnight, deep
glints of regret—why that night wafer in the sky never got close enough to lick,
or the grass there was no end to eating no matter how much
got swallowed, and how empty the brain with nothing to worship.
A head like this—whose long horns reel off greedily
toward inconsolable horizons; with nostrils so capacious
a soul could easily depart from one for a little out-of-bull escapade
and in one breath return through the other—a head like this,
the size of a small planet, could easily tire of pulling its body,
an entire universe of mystery, so that who could blame it
for one day lying down on the land and sighing,
with a big self-expelling snort, *Enough.*

Outside three white dogs begin at one end of the neighbor's yard
and run the slight length of it back and forth along the fence,
following a little dog on the other side the way particles follow a magnet.
Prancing and whirling, the little dog doesn't know its own power,
how maybe it had been a spirit on its way to divinity,
having learned the bigger lessons of pursuing hope, fleeing despair,
before getting stalled on the ground, thinking, What fun
to inhabit a little dog and chase around
not for money, or blood, no abracadabra,
just a good romp up and down the cyclone fence, not asking
why it's named for disaster, just dashing
and brushing the grass with the ease of a shadow.
The three dogs sound diminutive until the little dog replies
with a toy-piano rendition of bow-wow, wow-wow,

and although perhaps musically precocious, even the little dog knows nothing
of the bull floating in its first language—silence—which is also its last
and the last language of all the lost and all the scattered, and knows nothing
of the silence of bones and skulls,
the last of me, the last of you.

Sometimes Like the Ocean

In a dream turning like a clock of sand,
they called me a smuggler, for taking
what should have been left hidden.
The old boyfriend with blue eyes, black hair, carried
my mother down the beach after her attack
of blindness.
Someone else was trying to break
the owl bank by shaking it in a garbage can.
All I could think of were blue runway lights
and the feeling of flying when the ground
dissolves into clouds.
My mother called, but even in the dream
I knew she was not dying but dead.
The body has many holes, and we can be gone
from any one of them in an instant.
The white shore, as always, beckoned.
Lightning struck across the rippled bay,
rendering a young man speechless,
as mute as stars and the beacon on the fort
that blinked into the dark.
Here, gone, here, gone, the same
anxiety played out by waves that can never
leave the sand for long, the sand where the tides
hide the most illegal tender,
the blackest sand where I buried
what I could not carry.

Elsewhere

I wanted to write myself out of grief, dig out
to a place washed by heaven-haunted light,
the way a mad painter tunneled from his thatched hut
under the street to paint a Venezuelan beach.

Now, on another sand, boys throw rocks
at bullets and barricades.
Mothers ask, *Why close the roads to children?*
Mothers everywhere lower their heads and weep.

I can't imagine people in wartime, waking daily,
to white-hot recollections of not one but many deaths,
the names lancing though them over and over,
and the voice of God declaring, *Grind them to dust.*

What chance for small beauties—my mother's blue
hydrangeas, crates of pomegranates loaded with tart red jewels,
a newspaper whirling tirelessly in the underdraft of a truck
I followed for miles and miles of highway.

What chance these against the horror, that a government—mine—
could embark on "Operation Menu," its targets
called Breakfast, Lunch, Dinner, and Snacks, hellbent
on a diet of the dead.

Where is elsewhere?

The rain now casts a shawl of solitude over the day and I am left
writing into emphatic wet matter and the singular pain
of missing my mother, gone,
the way only she

        loved me.

Our Flowers

After the storm white and black clouds hung
in the sky like dogs and cats drinking
out of the same blue bowl.
It has been so long since we danced,
not counting the slow shuffle at the Zoo Ball,
you in the black tie the valet knotted in the parking lot
after the Internet instructions failed.
Failure is such a beautiful word for something
lousy, the lure of it not at all like the rain,
the drenching rain after the long hot drought that ended today.
When you said you loved substations, I thought of long
sandwiches until across the street I saw
the electricity-making equipment you'd already started
naming the parts of. I wanted to name the clouds—
dogwood, tiger lily, lilac, the lost flowers
of my girlhood, and of course the thousands of blossoms of phlox
in the rock garden my impossibly young grandmother sat in
for the photograph with three stone ducks.
What if we went back,
as children, to where no one asks how long the blooms
will bloom, to sleep with our grandmothers
in the feather bed carried from the old country,
all of us dreaming our own painful music, the songs
that will wake us in time for the next storm,
and even if it brings down limbs and live wires
dancing in wild arcs, we'll watch
the wind rouse the trees while the petals
of where we belong blow down
to rain on the unkissably muddy ground.

All

The prisoner can't go on any longer, but he does.
The beggar can't go on begging, but watch—
Tomorrow he'll be in the alley, holding out a bowl
To everyone, to even a young, possibly poorer, child.
The mother can't go on believing,
But she will kneel for hours in the cathedral,
Holding silence in her arms.
The rain goes on, daily, sometimes, and we cry,
As often as not alone.
The fishmonger, the bell ringer, the cook, each
Can be corrupted in a less than dire way.
Nothing can replace the sea breezes you were born to.
Nothing can stay the shy ache in the palm
you hold out to the fortune-teller.
The concrete lions on her steps go on
Making bloodless journeys, they go on
Hunting in air longer than any of you will live to watch,
Hunting still after your futures become all irises
and blamelessness.

Notes

p. 6   The quoted line, "The wind understands that to really suffer, one has to be faithful," is by the Polish poet Zbigniew Herbert.

p. 20   The *"philosophe"* is Brian Doyle, whose passage, "God writes death on all our hearts," I quote here.

p. 25   In the magazine *La Selva Subterránea*, Jorge Boccanera recounts a story told by the Costa Rican writer José Luís Sánchez. While imprisoned for murder at the island prison San Lucas, Luís Sánchez describes writing a letter on cement bags for a fellow inmate and how the letter weighed fifty pounds when he was done.

p. 30   "Pursuit" is for the Chinese painter Zhang Sheng, who I met at the Vermont Studio Center. In one of those happy cross-fertilizations afforded by a community of artists, his painting titles provided the stepping stones for the poem's narrative.

pp. 33–34 Quoted passages in "Clouds" come from *Savage Dreams: A Journey Into the Landscape Wars of the American West*, by Rebecca Solnit, in particular her writing on the nuclear wars waged by the government on the land and people of the western United States. The poem quotes her passage "the bomb and its quick and slow armageddons," as well as the physicist Mark Oliphant, who upon the successful detonation of the atom bomb, said, "This has been the death of a beautiful subject."

p. 37   The sheep image at the end of "History" is taken, with the kind permission of the author, from *Crossing Wildcat Ridge*, by Philip Lee Williams.

p. 46   "Damage" is for Emily Wheeler.

p. 48   "Gardens" is for Anna Zoë Rucker.

p. 54   "Secret Lives" is for Barbara, Ellen, Jenny, and Susanna.

p. 73   The Venezuelan painter referred to in the poem is Armando Reverón.

Barbara Ras is the author of *Bite Every Sorrow*, which won the Walt Whitman Award and the Kate Tufts Discovery Award. In 1999, she was nominated for the Southeastern Booksellers Association annual award in poetry and was named Georgia Poet of the Year. Ras's poems have appeared in *Boulevard, American Scholar, Orion, The Massachusetts Review, Georgia Review, TriQuarterly, Gulf Coast,* and other magazines and anthologies. She has received the Asher Montandon Award and honors from the National Writers Union, Villa Montalvo, San Jose Poetry Center, The Loft, and Bread Loaf Writers' Conference. She edited *Costa Rica: A Traveler's Literary Companion,* a collection of Costa Rican fiction in translation. Ras has taught in the Warren Wilson MFA Program for Writers and at workshops and conferences. She lives in San Antonio, Texas, where she directs Trinity University Press.

Penguin Poets

JOHN ASHBERY
Selected Poems
Self-Portrait in a Convex Mirror

TED BERRIGAN
The Sonnets

JIM CARROLL
Fear of Dreaming:
    The Selected Poems
Living at the Movies
Void of Course

ALISON HAWTHORNE DEMING
Genius Loci

CARL DENNIS
New and Selected Poems
    1974–2004
Practical Gods
Ranking the Wishes

DIANE DI PRIMA
Loba

STUART DISCHELL
Dig Safe

STEPHEN DOBYNS
Mystery, So Long
Velocities: New and Selected
    Poems: 1966–1992

AMY GERSTLER
Crown of Weeds
Ghost Girl
Nerve Storm

EUGENE GLORIA
Drivers at the Short-Time Motel
Hoodlum Birds

DEBORA GREGER
Desert Fathers, Uranium Daughters
God
Western Art

TERRANCE HAYES
Hip Logic
Wind in a Box

ROBERT HUNTER
Sentinel and Other Poems

MARY KARR
Viper Rum

JACK KEROUAC
Book of Blues
Book of Haikus
Book of Sketches

ANN LAUTERBACH
Hum
If in Time: Selected Poems,
    1975–2000
On a Stair

CORINNE LEE
PYX

PHYLLIS LEVIN
Mercury

WILLIAM LOGAN
Macbeth in Venice
Night Battle
The Whispering Gallery

MICHAEL MCCLURE
Huge Dreams: San Francisco
    and Beat Poems

DAVID MELTZER
David's Copy: The Selected Poems
    of David Meltzer

CAROL MUSKE
An Octave Above Thunder
Red Trousseau

ALICE NOTLEY
The Descent of Alette
Disobedience
Mysteries of Small Houses

BARBARA RAS
One Hidden Stuff

PATTIANN ROGERS
Generations

TRYFON TOLIDES
An Almost Pure Empty Walking

STEPHANIE STRICKLAND
V: WaveSon.nets/Losing L'una

ANNE WALDMAN
Kill or Cure
Marriage: A Sentence
Structure of the World
    Compared to a Bubble

JAMES WELCH
Riding the Earthboy 40

PHILIP WHALEN
Overtime: Selected Poems

ROBERT WRIGLEY
Earthly Meditations
Lives of the Animals
Reign of Snakes

MARK YAKICH
Unrelated Individuals Forming a
    Group Waiting to Cross

JOHN YAU
Borrowed Love Poems
Paradiso Diaspora